THE
SECRET DOOR
TO SUCCESS

T0143883

Also available in the Condensed Classics Library

~

A Message to Garcia
Acres of Diamonds
Alcoholics Anonymous
As a Man Thinketh
How to Attract Good Luck
How to Attract Money
Public Speaking to Win!
Self-Reliance
The Game of Life and How to Play It
The Kybalion
The Law of Success
The Magic Ladder to Success
The Magic of Believing
The Master Key to Riches
The Master Mind
The Million Dollar Secret Hidden in Your Mind
The Power of Concentration
The Power of Your Subconscious Mind
The Science of Being Great
The Science of Getting Rich
The Secret Door to Success
The Secret of the Ages
Think and Grow Rich
Your Faith Is Your Fortune

THE
SECRET DOOR
TO SUCCESS

by
Florence Scovel Shinn

Your Guide to Miraculous Living

Abridged and Introduced
by Mitch Horowitz

THE CONDENSED 📖 CLASSICS LIBRARY™

MEDIA

Published by Gildan Media LLC
aka G&D Media.
www.GandDmedia.com

The Secret Door to Success was originally published in 1940
G&D Media Condensed Classics edition published 2018
Abridgement and Introduction copyright © 2016 by Mitch
Horowitz

FIRST EDITION: 2018

Cover design by David Rheinhardt of Pyrographx

Interior design by Meghan Day Healey of Story Horse, LLC.

ISBN: 978-1-7225-0049-8

CONTENTS

INTRODUCTION
Last Testament of a Miracle Worker 7

CHAPTER ONE
The Secret Door to Success 11

CHAPTER TWO
Bricks Without Straw 17

CHAPTER THREE
"And Five of Them Were Wise" 21

CHAPTER FOUR
What Do You Expect? 25

CHAPTER FIVE
The Long Arm of God 29

CHAPTER SIX
The Fork in the Road...................................33

CHAPTER SEVEN
Crossing Your Red Sea..............................37

CHAPTER EIGHT
Look With Wonder...................................43

CHAPTER NINE
Rivers in the Desert................................49

ABOUT THE AUTHORS 55

Last Testament
of a Miracle Worker

This book almost never saw publication. It appeared in 1940, the year that Florence Scovel Shinn died. The work of the metaphysical teacher remains a formative influence on people around the world touched by her simple message that *thoughts are destiny*.

Shinn has many times over passed the test that philosopher Ralph Waldo Emerson posed for whether someone has lived well—which is "to know that even one life has breathed easier because you have lived." I believe that Shinn, through her message of mental causation, left many thousands of people breathing easier, and living better. She may be about to do the same for you.

Shinn is best known for her 1925 classic *The Game of Life and How to Play It*. While Shinn called life a "game," her own life was not easy—and nor did she seek ease. Born Florence Scovel in Camden, New Jersey in 1871, she took a rare path as a female artist, attending the Pennsylvania Academy of Fine Arts. There she met her future husband, realist painter Everett Shinn. Married in 1898, they moved to New York's Greenwich Village, where they became part of the Ashcan School of American artists, a cohort known for depicting street scenes, tenements, and the immigrant experience. The couple divorced in 1912. While pursuing her own career as an illustrator, Shinn became a student of metaphysics, leading her to write *The Game of Life* and several other books. She also became a popular spiritual lecturer and counselor. Following an illness, she died at home in Manhattan in October of 1940.

Shinn provided a role model for many independent seekers not only by how she lived out her principles of self-creation, but also by her do-it-yourself ethic. When no publisher would accept her manuscript for *The Game of Life*, Shinn published the book herself. It became one of the most popular works of practical metaphysics of the past hundred years, and remains widely read today. She did the same with her next book, *Your Word is Your Wand*, published in 1928, and with this one. The final book that bears her name, *The Power of the Spoken Word*, appeared posthumously in 1944, four years after her death.

The Secret Door to Success uses the Bible as its chief point of reference. This has been a basic aspect of New Thought tradition. Shinn and her contemporaries interpreted Scripture as a psychological blueprint of individual development and personal excellence. In so doing, Shinn influenced some of the most powerful and varied voices in the positive-mind tradition, including the mystic Neville Goddard and the mega-selling Norman Vincent Peale, both of whom used Shinn's phraseology in her work. Shinn was likewise an influence on spiritual thinkers of our own generation, including writer-publisher Louise Hay and on Yolanda King, eldest daughter of Martin Luther King Jr.

Shinn's contemporary Emmet Fox eulogized her: "One secret of Shinn's success was that she was always herself . . . colloquial, informal, friendly, and humorous. She never sought to be literary, conventional, or impressive. For this reason she appealed to thousands who would not have taken the spiritual message through more conservative and dignified forms, or have been willing to read . . . at least in the beginning . . . the standard metaphysical books."

I quote from Fox's eulogy with a tinge of hesitancy. There is, I think, something of a backhanded compliment, or even a veiled putdown, in his noting that Shinn's books are for seekers who might not have taken the message through more "dignified forms." A problem with our spiritual and intellectual culture (and many of those who aspire to be a part of it) is its suspicion of simple ideas and methods.

Shinn's technique of "speaking the word"—of placing faith in God's channels and announcing the arrival of that which is needed—either works or it does not. If it works—and I say that, in great measure, it does and challenge the reader to find his or her own applications—where is the need for the more "dignified" works to which Fox alludes? We should never be embarrassed or warned off an idea because it is simple. The only true test of a religious or ethical principle is its efficacy. That may be why Shinn is far more widely read today than Fox and many of her contemporaries.

Shinn's natural, practical voice inspired a wide range of seekers and metaphysical ministers. In so doing, she gave New Thought its popular tone: one of encouragement, experiment, boldness, and boundless possibility. In this, the final book of Shinn's life, now a part of our Condensed Classics Library, the teacher left us a testament that conveys something of the woman herself.

—Mitch Horowitz

CHAPTER ONE

The Secret Door to Success

"So the people shouted when the priests blew with the trumpets; and it came to pass, when the people heard the sound of the trumpet, and the people shouted with a great shout, that the wall fell down flat, so that the people went up into the city, every man straight before him, and they took the city." —JOSHUA 6:20

A successful man is always asked—"What is the secret of your success?"

People never ask a man who is a failure, "What is the secret of your failure?" It is quite easy to see and they are not interested.

People all want to know how to open the secret door to success.

For each man there is success, but it seems to be behind a door or wall. In the Bible reading, we have heard the wonderful story of the falling of the walls of Jericho.

Of course all biblical stories have a metaphysical interpretation.

We will talk now about *your* wall of Jericho: the wall separating *you* from success. Nearly everyone has built a wall around his own Jericho.

This city you are not able to enter, contains great treasures; your divinely designed success, your heart's desire!

What kind of wall have you built around your Jericho? Often, it is a wall of resentment—resenting someone, or resenting a situation, shuts off your good.

If you are a failure and resent the success of someone else, you are keeping away your own success.

I have given the following statement to neutralize envy and resentment: *What God has done for others, He now does for me and more.*

I gave the following statement to a woman: *The walls of lack and delay now crumble away, and I enter my Promised Land, under grace.* She had a vivid picture of stepping over a fallen wall, and received the demonstration of her good, almost immediately.

It is the word of realization that brings about a change in your affairs; for words and thoughts are a form of radioactivity.

Taking an interest in your work, enjoying what you are doing opens the secret door of success.

The *Secret of Success is to make what you are doing interesting to other people.* Be interested yourself, and others will find you interesting.

A good disposition, a smile, often opens the secret door; the Chinese say, "A man without a smiling face, must not open a shop."

Living in the past, complaining of your misfortunes, builds a thick wall around your Jericho.

Talking too much about your affairs, scattering your forces, brings you up against a high wall. I knew a man of brains and ability, who was a complete failure.

He lived with his mother and aunt, and I found that every night when he went home to dinner, he told them all that had taken place during the day at the office; he discussed his hopes, his fears, and his failures.

I said to him, "You scatter your forces by talking about your affairs. Don't discuss your business with your family. Silence is golden!"

Success is not a secret, it is a System.

Many people are up against the wall of discouragement. Courage and endurance are part of the system. We read this in lives of all successful men and women.

Only twice is the word success mentioned in the Bible—both times in the Book of Joshua.

"Only be strong and very courageous to observe to do according to all the law which Moses, my servant, commanded thee: turn not from it to the right nor to the left, that thou mayest have good success whithersoever thou goest. This book of the law shall not depart from thy mouth, but thou shalt meditate therein day and night, that thou mayest observe to do all that is written therein, for then shalt thou make thy way prosperous and thou shalt have good success. Turn not to the right nor to the left."

The *road to success is a straight and narrow path; it is a road of loving absorption, of undivided attention.*

"You attract the things you give a great deal of thought to."

So if you give a great deal of thought to lack, you attract lack, if you give a great deal of thought to injustice, you attract more injustice.

Joshua said, "And it shall come to pass, that when they make a long blast with the ram's horn, and when ye hear the sound of the trumpet, all the people shall shout with a great shout: and the wall of the city shall fall down flat, and the people shall ascend up, every man straight before him."

The inner meaning of this story is the power of the word, your word, which dissolves obstacles and removes barriers.

When the people shouted the walls fell down.

We find in folklore and fairy stories, which come down from legends founded on Truth, the same idea—a word opens a door or cleaves a rock.

So let us now take the statement—The walls of lack and delay now crumble away, and I enter my Promised Land, under grace.

CHAPTER TWO

Bricks Without Straw

"There shall no straw be given you, yet ye shall make bricks without straw." —EXODUS 5:18

I n the fifth chapter of Exodus, we have a picture of every day life, when giving a metaphysical interpretation.

The Children of Israel were in bondage to Pharaoh, the cruel taskmaster, ruler of Egypt. They were kept in slavery, making bricks, and were hated and despised.

Moses had orders from the Lord to deliver his people from bondage—"Moses and Aaron went in and told Pharaoh—Thus saith the Lord God of Israel, Let my people go, that they may hold a feast unto me in the wilderness."

He not only refused to let them go, but told them he would make their tasks even more difficult: they must make bricks without straw being provided for them.

It was impossible to make bricks without straw. The Children of Israel were completely crushed by Pharaoh; they were beaten for not producing the bricks—then came the message from Jehovah.

"Go therefore now, and work; for there shall no straw be given you, yet shall ye deliver the tale (number) of bricks."

I was told the story of a woman who needed money for her rent. It was necessary to have it at once, but she knew of no channel, she exhausted every avenue.

However, she was a Truth student, and kept making her affirmations. Her dog whined and wanted to go out, she put on his leash and walked down the street, in the accustomed direction.

However, the dog pulled at his leash and wanted to go in another direction.

She followed, and in the middle of the block, opposite an open park, she looked down, and picked up a roll of bills, which exactly covered her rent.

She looked for ads, but never found the owner. There were no houses near where she found it.

The reasoning mind, the intellect, takes the throne of Pharaoh in your consciousness. It says continually, "It can't be done. What's the use!"

We must drown out these dreary suggestions with a vital affirmation!

For example take this statement: *"The unexpected happens, my seemingly impossible good now comes to pass."* This stops all argument from the army of the aliens (the reasoning mind.).

"The unexpected happens!" That is an idea it cannot cope with.

Think of the joy of really being free forever, from the Pharaoh of the oppression. To have the idea of *security, health, happiness and abundance established in the subconscious*. It would mean a life free from all limitation!

It would be the Kingdom that Jesus Christ spoke of, where all things are automatically added unto us. I say automatically added unto us, because all life is vibration; and when we vibrate to success, happiness and abundance, the things that symbolize these states of consciousness will attach themselves to us.

Feel rich and successful, and suddenly you receive a large check or a beautiful gift.

CHAPTER THREE

"And Five of Them Were Wise"

*"And five of them were wise, and five were fool-
ish. They that were foolish took their lamps, and
took no oil with them."* —MATT. 25:2–3

My subject is the parable of the Wise and Foolish Virgins. "And five of them were wise, and
five were foolish. They that were foolish took
their lamps, and took no oil with them. But the wise
took oil in their vessels with their lamps." The parable
teaches that true prayer means preparation.

Jesus Christ said, "And all things, whatsoever ye
shall ask in prayer, *believing*, ye shall receive" (Matt.
21:22). "Therefore I say unto you, what things soever ye
desire, when ye pray, believe that ye receive them, and
ye shall have them" (Mark 11:24). In this parable he

shows that only those who have prepared for their good (thereby showing active faith) will bring the manifestation to pass.

We might paraphrase the scriptures and say: When you pray believe you have it. When you pray ACT as if you have already received.

Armchair faith or rocking chair faith will never move mountains. In the armchair, in the silence, or meditation, you are filled with the wonder of this Truth, and feel that your faith will never waver. You know that The Lord is your Shepherd, you shall never want.

You feel that your God of Plenty will wipe out all burdens of debt or limitations, then you leave your armchair and step out into the arena of Life. It is only what you do in the arena that counts.

I will you give you an illustration showing how the law works; for faith without action is dead.

A man, one of my students, had a great desire to go abroad. He took the statement: *I give thanks for my divinely designed trip, divinely financed, under grace, in a perfect way.* He had very little money, but knowing the law of preparation, he bought a trunk. It was a very happy trunk with a big red band around its waist. Whenever he looked at it it gave him a realization of a trip. One day he seemed to feel his room moving. He felt the motion of a ship. He went to the window to breathe the fresh air, and it smelt like the aroma of the docks. With his inner ear he heard the shriek of a seagull and the creaking of the gangplank. The trunk had commenced to work. It had put him in the vibration of his trip. Soon after that, a large sum of money came to him and he took the trip. He said afterwards that it was perfect in every detail.

In the arena of Life we must keep ourselves tuned-up to concert pitch.

Are we acting from motives of fear or faith? *Watch your motives with all diligence, for out of them are the issues of life.*

The lamp symbolizes man's consciousness. The oil is what brings Light or understanding.

"While the bridegroom tarried, they all slumbered and slept. And at midnight there was a cry made. Behold, the bridegroom cometh; go ye out to meet him. Then all those virgins arose, and trimmed their lamps. And the foolish said unto the wise, "Give us of your oil; for our lamps are gone out."

The foolish virgins were without wisdom or understanding, which is oil for the consciousness, and when they were confronted with a serious situation, they had no way of handling it.

And when they said to the wise "give us of your oil," the wise answered saying, "Not so; lest there be not enough for us and you: but go ye rather to them that sell, and buy for yourselves."

That means that the foolish virgins could *not receive more than was in their consciousness, or what they were vibrating to.*

Every day you must make a choice, will you be wise or foolish? Will you prepare for your good? Will you *take the giant swing into faith*? Or serve doubt and fear and bring no oil for your lamps?

Every day examine your consciousness and see just what you are preparing for. You are fearful of lack and hang on to every cent, thereby attracting more lack. Use what you have with wisdom and it opens the way for more to come to you.

CHAPTER FOUR

What Do You Expect?

"According to your faith, be it done unto you."
—MATT. 9:29

Faith is expectancy—"According to your faith, be it done unto you."

We might say, according to your expectancies be it done unto you. So, what are you expecting?

We hear people say: "We expect the worst to happen," or "The worst is yet to come." They are deliberately inviting the worst to come.

We hear others say: "I expect a change for the better." They are inviting better conditions into their lives.

Change your expectancies and you change your conditions.

How can you change your expectancies, when you have formed the habit of expecting loss, lack or failure?

Begin to act as if you expected success, happiness, and abundance; *prepare for your good*.

Do something to show you expect it to come. Active faith alone will impress the subconscious.

If you have spoken the word for a home, prepare for it immediately, as if you hadn't a moment to lose. Collect little ornaments, tablecloths, etc., etc.!

I knew a woman who made the giant swing into faith, by buying a large armchair; a chair meant business, she bought a large and comfortable chair, for she was preparing for the right man. He came.

Someone will say, "Suppose you haven't money to buy ornaments or a chair?" Then look in shop windows and link with them in thought.

Get in their vibration: I sometimes hear people say, "I don't go into the shops because I can't afford to buy anything." That is just the reason why you should go into the shops. Begin to make friends with the things you desire or require.

I know a woman who wanted a ring. She went boldly to the ring department and tried on rings. It gave her such a realization of ownership, that not long after, a friend made her a gift of a ring. "You combine with what you notice."

The soul is the subconscious mind, and the psalmist was telling his subconscious to expect everything directly from the universal; not to depend upon doors and channels; "My expectation is from Him."

God cannot fail, for "His ways are ingenious, His methods are sure."

You can expect any seemingly impossible Good from God; if you do not limit the channels.

Do not say how you want it done, or how it can't be done.

"God is the Giver and the Gift *and creates His own amazing channels.*"

Now think of the blessings that seem so far off, and begin to expect them now, under grace, in an unexpected way; for God works in unexpected ways, His wonders to perform.

CHAPTER FIVE

The Long Arm of God

"The Eternal God is thy refuge, and underneath are the everlasting arms." —DEUT. 33:27

Have you ever felt the relief of getting out some negative thought-form? Perhaps you have built up a thought-form of resentment, until you are always boiling with anger about something. You resent people you know, people you don't know, people in the past, and people in the present, and you may be sure that the people in the future won't escape your wrath.

All the organs of the body are affected by resentment—for when you resent, you resent with every organ of the body.

I have given the following statement to many of my students: *The long arm of God reaches out over people*

*and conditions, controlling this situation and protecting
my interests.*

This brings a picture of a long arm symbolizing
strength and protection. With the realization of the
power of the long arm of God, you would no longer
resist or resent. You would relax and let go. The enemy
thoughts within you would be destroyed, therefore, *the
adverse conditions would disappear.*

Spiritual development means the ability to stand
still, or stand aside, and let Infinite Intelligence lift your
burdens and fight your battles. When the burden of resentment is lifted, you experience a sense of relief! You
have a kindly feeling for everyone, and all the organs of
your body begin to function properly.

Non-resistance is an art. When acquired, The
World is Yours! So many people are trying to force sit-
uations. Your lasting good will never comes through
forcing personal will.

> *Flee from the things which flee from thee*
> *Seek nothing, fortune seeketh thee.*
> *Behold his shadow on the floor!*
> *Behold him standing at the door!*

I do not know the author of these lines. Lovelock,
the celebrated English athlete, was asked how to attain

his speed and endurance in running. He replied, "Learn to relax." Let us attain this rest in action. He was most relaxed when running the fastest.

Your big opportunity and big success usually slide in, when you least expect it. You have to let go long enough for the *great law of attraction to operate. You never saw a worried and anxious magnet.* It stands up straight and hasn't a care in the world, because it knows needles can't help jumping to it. The things we rightly desire come to pass when we have taken the clutch off.

Do not let your heart's desire become your heart's disease. You are completely demagnetized when you desire something too intensely. You worry, fear, and agonize. There is an occult law of indifference: "None of these things move me." Your ships come in over a don't-care sea.

So many people use their words in exaggerated and reckless statements. I find a great deal of material for my talks in the beauty parlor. A young girl wanted a magazine to read. She called to the operator, "Give me something terribly new and frightfully exciting." All she wanted was the latest moving picture magazine. You hear people say, "I wish something terribly exciting would happen." They are inviting some unhappy, but exciting, experience into their lives. Then they wonder why it happened to them.

There should be a chair of metaphysics in all colleges. *Metaphysics is the wisdom of the ages.* It is the ancient wisdom taught all through the centuries in India and Egypt and Greece. Hermes Trismegistus was a great teacher of Egypt. His teachings were closely guarded and have come down to us over ten centuries. He lived in Egypt in the days when the present race of men was in its infancy. But if you read *The Kybalion* carefully, you find that he taught just what we are teaching today. He said that all mental states were accompanied by vibrations. You combine with what you vibrate to, so let us all now vibrate to success, happiness, and abundance.

Now is the appointed time. Today is the day of my amazing good fortune.

Chapter Six

The Fork in the Road

"Choose you this day whom ye will serve."
—Josh. 24:15

Every day there is a necessity of choice—a fork in the road.

"Shall I do this, or shall I do that? Shall I go, or shall I stay?" Many people do not know what to do. They rush about letting other people make decisions for them, then regret having taken their advice.

There are others who carefully reason things out. They weigh and measure the situation like dealing in groceries, and are surprised when they fail to obtain their goal.

There are still other people who follow the magic path of intuition and find themselves in their Promised Land in the twinkling of an eye.

Intuition is a spiritual faculty high above the reasoning mind, but on the path is all that you desire or require.

So choose ye this day to follow the magic path of intuition.

In my question-and-answer classes I describe how to cultivate intuition. In most people it is a faculty that has remained dormant. So we say, "Awake thou that sleepeth. Wake up to your leads and hunches. Wake up to the divinity within!"

Claude Bragdon said, "To live intuitively is to live fourth dimensionally."

Now, it is necessary for you to make a decision, you face a fork in the road. *Ask for a definite unmistakable lead*, and you will receive it.

We find many events to interpret metaphysically in the Book of Joshua. "After the death of Moses, the divine command came to Joshua, 'Now therefore, arise, go over the Jordan, thou and all thy people, unto the land which I do give to them. Every place the sole of your feet shall tread upon; to you have I given it'."

The feet are the symbol of understanding, so it means metaphysically all that we understand stands under us in consciousness, and what is rooted there can never be taken from us.

For, the Bible goes on to say: "There shall not any man be able to stand before thee all the days of thy life . . . I will not fail thee, nor forsake thee. Only be thou strong and very courageous, that thou mayest observe to do according to all the law, which Moses my servant commanded thee: 'turn not from it to the right hand or to the left, that thou mayest prosper whithersoever thou goest'."

So we find we have success through being strong and very courageous in following spiritual law. We are back again to the "fork in the road"—the necessity of choice.

"Choose you this day whom ye will serve," the intellect or divine guidance.

So, as we reach the fork in the road today, let us fearlessly follow the voice of intuition.

The Bible calls it "the still small voice."

"There came a voice behind me, saying, 'This is the way, walk ye in it'." On this path is the good, already prepared for you. You will find the "land for which ye did not labor, and cities which ye built not, and ye dwell in them; of the vineyards and olive yards which ye planted not, do ye eat."

Let us say: *I am divinely led, I follow the right fork in the road. God makes a way where there is no way.*

Chapter Seven

Crossing Your Red Sea

"Speak unto the children of Israel that they go forward." —Ex. 14:15

One of the most dramatic stories in the Bible is the episode of the children of Israel crossing the Red Sea.

Moses was leading them out of the land of Egypt where they were kept in bondage and slavery. They were being pursued by the Egyptians.

The children of Israel, like most people, did not enjoy trusting God; they did a lot of murmuring. They said to Moses: "Is not this the word that we did tell thee in Egypt, saying, Let us alone, that we may serve the Egyptians? For it had been better for us to serve the Egyptians, than that we should die in the wilderness."

"And Moses said unto the people, Fear ye not, stand still, and see the salvation of the Lord, which he will show to you today, for the Egyptians whom ye have seen today, ye shall see them again no more forever."

"The Lord shall fight for you, and ye shall hold your peace."

We might say that Moses pounded faith into the children of Israel.

They preferred being slaves to their old doubts and fears (for Egypt stands for darkness), than to take the giant swing into faith, and pass through the wilderness to their Promised Land.

There is, indeed, a wilderness to pass through before your Promised Land is reached.

The old doubts and fears encamp round about you, but there is always someone to tell you to go forward! There is always a Moses on your pathway. Sometimes it is a friend, sometimes intuition!

"And the Lord said to Moses, Wherefore cryest thou unto me? Speak unto the children of Israel, that *they go forward!*"

Now remember, the bible is talking about the individual. It is talking about *your* wilderness, *your* Red Sea, and *your* Promised Land.

Each one of you has a Promised Land, a heart's desire, but you have been so enslaved by the Egyptians (your negative thoughts), it seems very far away, and too good to be true. You consider trusting God a very risky proposition. The wilderness might prove worse than the Egyptians. And how do you know your Promised Land really exists?

The reasoning mind will always back up the Egyptians.

But sooner or later, something says, *"Go forward!"* It is usually circumstances—you are driven to it.

I give the example of a student. She is a very marvelous pianist and had great success abroad. She came back with a book full of press clippings, and a happy heart.

A relative took an interest in her and said she would back her financially for a concert tour. They chose a manager who took charge of the expenses, and attended to her bookings.

After a concert or two, there were no more funds. The manager had taken them. My friend was left stranded, desolate, and disappointed. This was about the time that she came to me.

She hated the man, and it was making her ill. She had very little money and could afford only a cheerless room where her hands were often too cold to practice.

She was indeed, in bondage to the Egyptians— hate, resentment, lack, and limitation.

Someone brought her to one of my meetings, and she spoke to me and told her story. I said, "In the first place you must stop hating that man. When you are able to forgive him, your success will come back to you. You are taking your initiation in forgiveness."

It seemed a pretty big order, but she tried and came regularly to all my meetings.

In the meantime, the relative had started a suit to recover the money. Time went on and it never came to court.

My friend had a call to go to California. She was no longer disturbed by the situation, and had forgiven the man.

Suddenly, after about four years, she was notified that the case had come to court. She called me upon her arrival in New York, and asked me to speak the word for rightness and justice.

They went at the time appointed, and it was all settled out of court, the man restoring the money by monthly payments.

She came to me overflowing with joy, for she said, "I hadn't the least resentment toward the man. He was amazed when I greeted him cordially." Her relative said that all the money was to go to her, so she found herself with a big bank account.

Now she will soon reach her Promised Land. She came out of the house of bondage (of hate and resentment) and crossed her Red Sea. Her goodwill toward the man caused the waters to part, and she crossed over on dry land.

CHAPTER EIGHT

Look With Wonder

"I will remember the works of the Lord; surely I will remember thy wonders of old."

—PSALMS 77:11

The words wonder and wonderful are used many times in the Bible. In the dictionary the word wonder is defined as, "a cause for surprise, astonishment, a miracle, a marvel."

P.D. Ouspensky, in his book *Tertium Organum*, calls the 4th dimensional world, the "World of the Wondrous." He has figured out mathematically that there is a realm where all conditions are perfect. Jesus Christ called it the Kingdom.

We might say, "Seek ye first the world of the wondrous, and all things shall be added unto you."

It can only be reached through a state of consciousness.

Jesus Christ said to enter the Kingdom we must become "as a little child." Children are continually in a state of joy and wonder!

The future holds promises of mysterious good. Anything can happen overnight.

Robert Louis Stevenson in *A Child's Garden of Verses* says: "The world is so full of a number of things. I'm sure we should all be as happy as kings."

So let us look with wonder at that which is before us. That statement was given me a number of years ago, I mention it in my book, *The Game of Life and How To Play It*.

I had missed an opportunity and felt that I should have been more awake to my good. The next day, I took the statement early in the morning: "I look with wonder at that which is before me."

At noon the phone rang, and the proposition was put to me again. This time I grasped it. I did indeed look with wonder for I never expected the opportunity to come to me again.

A friend in one of my meetings said the other day that this statement had brought her wonderful results. It fills the consciousness with happy expectancy.

Children are filled with happy expectancy until grown-up people, and unhappy experiences, bring them out of the world of the wondrous!

Let us look back and remember some of the gloomy ideas that were given us: "Eat the speckled apples first." "Don't expect too much, then you won't be disappointed." "You can't have everything in this life." "Childhood is your happiest time." "No one knows what the future will bring."

These are some of the impressions I picked up in early childhood.

At the age of six I had a great sense of responsibility. Instead of looking with wonder at that which was before me, I looked with fear and suspicion. I feel much younger now than I did when I was six.

I have an early photograph taken about that time, grasping a flower, but with a careworn and hopeless expression.

I had left the world of the wondrous behind me! I was now living in the world of realities, as my elders told me, and it was far from wondrous.

It is a great privilege for children to live in this age, when they are taught Truth from their birth. Even if they are not taught actual metaphysics, the ethers are filled with joyous expectancy.

So let us become *Miracle Conscious* and prepare for miracles, expect miracles, and we are then inviting them into our lives.

Maybe you need a financial miracle! There is a supply for every demand. Through active faith, the word, and intuition, we release this invisible supply.

I will give an example: One of my students found herself almost without funds, she needed one thousand dollars, and she had had plenty of money at one time and beautiful possessions, but had nothing left but an ermine wrap. No fur dealer would give her much for it.

I spoke the word that it would be sold to the right person for the right price, or that the supply would come in some other way. It was necessary that the money manifest at once, it was no time to worry or reason.

She was on the street making her affirmations. It was a stormy day. She said to herself, "I'm going to show active faith in my invisible supply by taking a taxi cab." It was a very strong hunch. As she got out of the taxi, at her destination, a woman stood waiting to get in.

It was an old friend, a very, very kind friend. It was the first time in her life she had ever taken a taxi, but her Rolls Royce was out of commission that afternoon.

They talked and my friend told her about the ermine wrap. "Why," her friend said, "I will give you a thousand dollars for it." And that afternoon she had the check.

God's ways are ingenious, His methods are sure.

CHAPTER NINE

Rivers in the Desert

"Behold, I will do a new thing: now it shall spring forth; shall ye not know it? I will even make a way in the wilderness, and rivers in the desert."
—ISAIAH 43:19

In this 43rd chapter of Isaiah are many wonderful statements, showing the irresistible power of Supreme Intelligence coming to man's rescue in times of trouble. *No matter how impossible the situation seems, Infinite Intelligence knows the way out.*

Working with God-Power, man becomes unconditioned and absolute. Let us get a realization of this hidden power that we can call upon at any moment.

Make your contact with Infinite Intelligence (the God within) and all appearance of evil evaporates, for it comes from man's "vain imaginings."

In my question-and-answer class I would be asked, "How do you make a conscious contact with this Invincible Power?"

I reply, "By your word." "By your word you are justified."

The Centurion said to Jesus Christ, "Speak the word, master and my servant shall be healed."

"Whosoever calleth on the name of the Lord shall be delivered." Notice the word, "call:" you are calling on the Lord or Law, when you make an affirmation of Truth.

As I always say, take a statement that "clicks," that means, gives you a feeling of security.

People are enslaved by ideas of lack: lack of love, lack of money, lack of companionship, lack of health, and so on.

They are enslaved by the ideas of interference and incompletion. They are asleep in the Adamic Dream: Adam (generic man) ate of "Maya the tree of illusion" and saw two powers, good and evil.

The Christ mission was to wake people up to the Truth of one power, God. "Awake thou that sleepeth."

If you lack any good thing, you are still asleep to your good.

How do you awake from the Adamic dream of opposites, after having slept soundly in the race thought for hundreds of years?

Jesus Christ said, "When two of you agree, it shall be done." It is the law of agreement.

It is almost impossible to see clearly, your good, for yourself: that is where the healer, practitioner or friend is necessary.

Most successful men say they have succeeded because their wives believed in them. I will quote from a current newspaper, giving Walter P. Chrysler's tribute to his wife, "Nothing," he once said, "has given me more satisfaction in life, than the way my wife had faith in me from the very first, through all those years." Chrysler wrote of her, "It seemed to me I could not make anyone understand that I was ambitious except Della. I could tell her and she would nod. It seems to me I even dared to tell her that I intended, some day, to be a master mechanic." She always backed his ambitions.

Talk about your affairs as little as possible, and then only to the ones who will give you encouragement and inspiration. The world is full of "wet blankets," people who will tell you "it can't be done," that "you are aiming too high."

As people sit in Truth meetings and services, often a word or an idea will open a way in the wilderness.

Of course the Bible is speaking of states of consciousness. You are in a wilderness or desert, when you are out of harmony—when you are angry, resentful, fearful or undecided. Indecision is the cause of much ill health, being unable "to make up your mind."

One day when I was on a bus a woman stopped it and asked the conductor its destination. He told her, but she was undecided. She got half way on, and then got off, then on again: the conductor turned to her and said, "Lady, make up your mind!"

So it is with so many people—"Make up your minds!"

The intuitive person is never undecided: he is given his leads and hunches, and goes boldly ahead, knowing he is on the magic path.

In Truth, we always ask for definite leads just what to do; you will always receive one if you ask for it. Sometimes it comes as intuition, sometimes from the external.

One of my students, named Ada, was walking down the street, undecided whether to go to a certain place or not. She asked for a lead. Two women were walking in front of her. One turned to the other and said, "Why don't you go Ada?"—the woman's name just happened to be Ada—my friend took it as a definite lead, and went on to her destination, and the outcome was very successful.

We really lead magic lives, guided and provided for at every step; *if we have ears to hear and eyes that see.*

Of course we have left the plane of the intellect and are drawing from the superconscious, the God within, which says, "This is the way, walk ye in it."

Whatever you should know, will be revealed to you. Whatever you lack, will be provided! "Thus saith the Lord which maketh a way in the sea and a path in the mighty waters."

"Remember ye not the former things, neither consider the things of old."

People who live in the past have severed their contact with the wonderful now. God knows only the *now*. Now is the appointed time, today is the day.

You must live in the now and be wide awake to your opportunities.

"Behold, I will do a new thing, now it shall spring forth; shall ye not know it? I will even make a way in the wilderness, and rivers in the desert."

This message is meant for the individual. Think of your problem and know that Infinite Intelligence knows the way of fulfillment. I say the *way*, for before you called you were answered. *The supply always precedes the demand.*

God is the Giver and the Gift and now creates His own amazing channels.

When you have asked for the Divine Plan of your life to manifest, you are protected from getting the things that are not in the Divine Plan.

You may think that all your happiness depends upon obtaining one particular thing in life; later on, you praise the Lord that you didn't get it.

Sometimes you are tempted to follow the reasoning mind, and argue with your intuitive leads, suddenly the Hand of Destiny pushes you into your right place, and under grace, you find yourself back on the magic path again.

You are now wide awake to your good—you have the ears that hear (your intuitive leads), and the eyes that see the open road of fulfillment.

The genius within me is released. I now fulfill my destiny.

Printed in the USA
CPSIA information can be obtained
at www.ICGtesting.com
JSHW012046140824
68134JS00034B/3291

9 781722 500498